the Garfield Gallery 1

Jim Davis

ЯR
RAVETTE BOOKS

First published by Ravette Books Limited 1992

Printed and bound for Ravette Books Limited
3 Glenside Estate, Star Road,
Partridge Green, Nr. Horsham,
West Sussex RH13 8RA
An Egmont Company
by STIGE, Italy

ISBN 1 85304 394 X

IT'S NICE TO BE LIKED JUST THE WAY YOU ARE

NEVER TRUST A SMILING CAT

JIM DAVIS

EVERYONE SHOULD LEARN
A FOREIGN LANGUAGE

Reach out
and touch
someone!

Welcome to the Funny Farm

JIM DAVIS

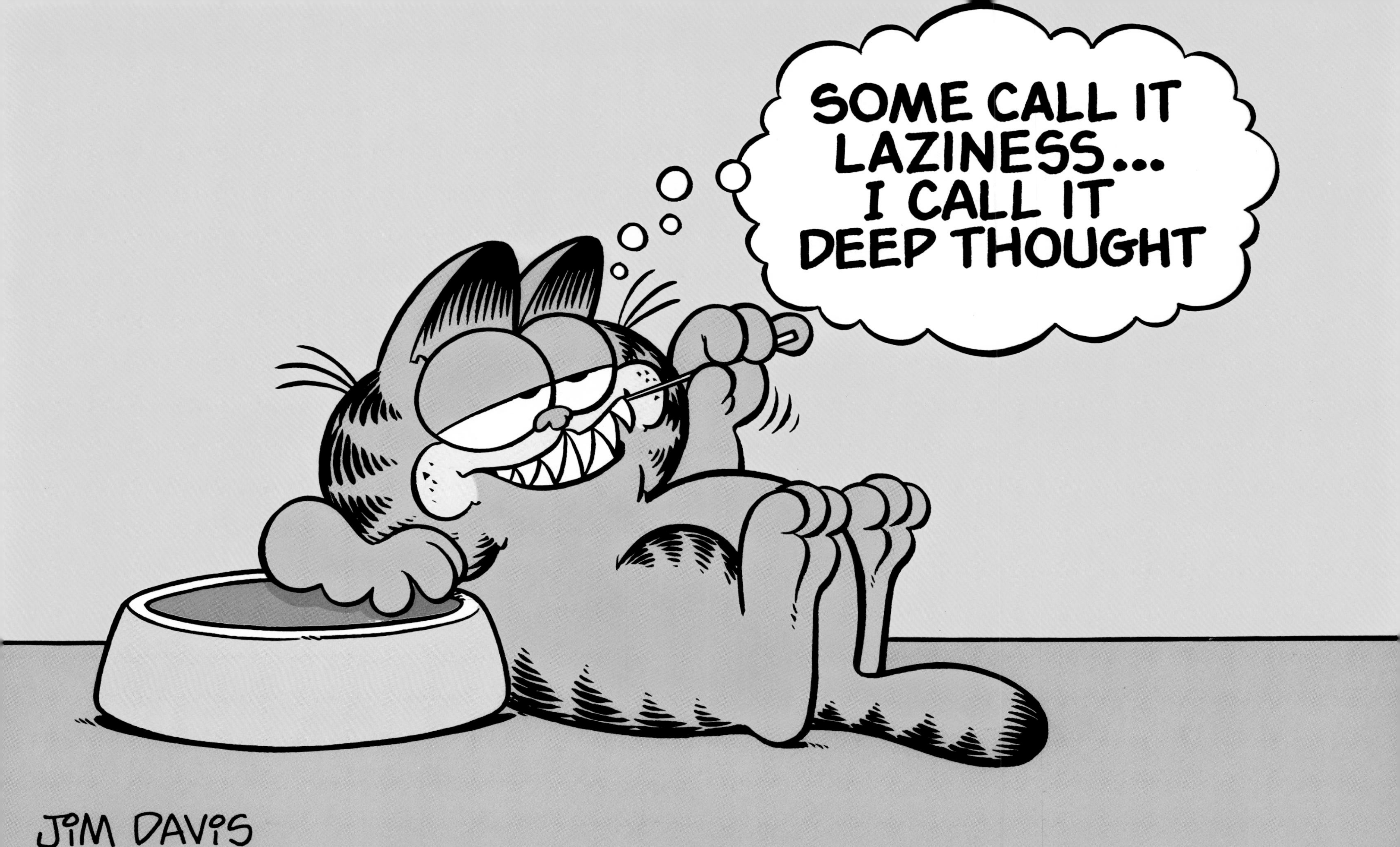
SOME CALL IT LAZINESS... I CALL IT DEEP THOUGHT
JIM DAVIS

© 1983 United Feature Syndicate, Inc.

3-6

For every action there is an equal and opposite reaction

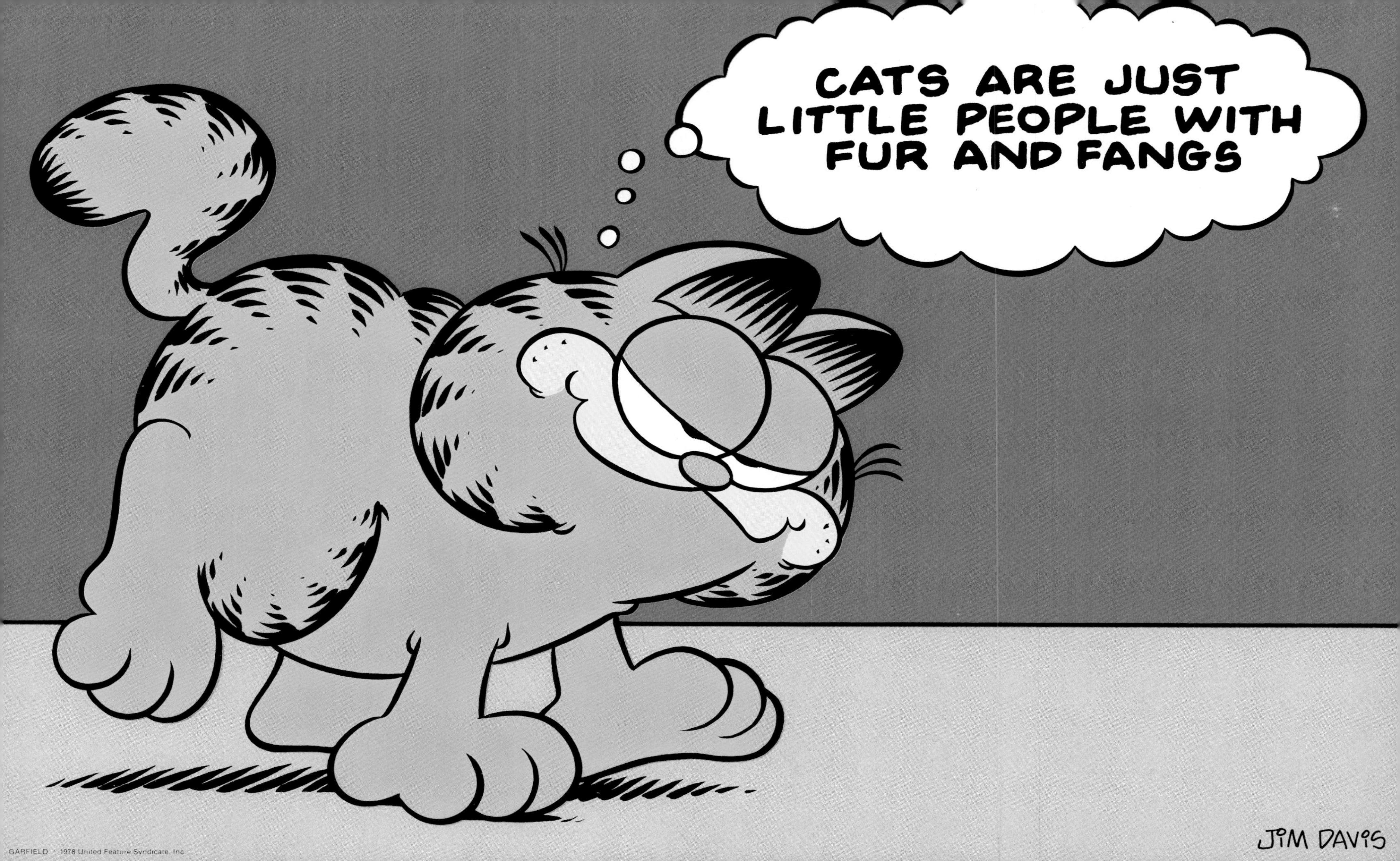
CATS ARE JUST LITTLE PEOPLE WITH FUR AND FANGS
JIM DAVIS

THE GARFIELD ANATOMY CHART

CHARLES ATLAS, EAT YOUR HEART OUT

CAN OPENER SENSORS

PASTA SPOTTERS

SMIRK

SMIRK RETAINERS

LASAGNA STORAGE UNITS

DAISY SNIFFER

HAIRBALL CATCHER

FURNITURE SHREDDERS

COB WEB COLLECTORS

STROKING SURFACE

SUNBEAM SOLAR PANEL

TWITCHER

WINDOW SILL PERCH

BEGGING PERCHES

JIM DAVIS

An active imagination is a wonderful thing